Holidays
Independence Day

by Erika S. Manley

Bullfrog Books

Ideas for Parents and Teachers

Bullfrog Books let children practice reading informational text at the earliest reading levels. Repetition, familiar words, and photo labels support early readers.

Before Reading

- Discuss the cover photo. What does it tell them?
- Look at the picture glossary together. Read and discuss the words.

Read the Book

- "Walk" through the book and look at the photos. Let the child ask questions. Point out the photo labels.
- Read the book to the child, or have him or her read independently.

After Reading

- Prompt the child to think more. Ask: Do you celebrate Independence Day? What do you do?

Bullfrog Books are published by Jump!
5357 Penn Avenue South
Minneapolis, MN 55419
www.jumplibrary.com

Library of Congress Cataloging-in-Publication Data

Names: Manley, Erika S., author.
Title: Independence Day / by Erika S. Manley.
Description: Minneapolis, Minnesota: Jump! Inc., 2018. | Series: Holidays | Includes index.
Identifiers: LCCN 2017022925 (print)
LCCN 2017027861 (ebook) | ISBN 9781624966651 (ebook) | ISBN 9781620318324 (hardcover: alkaline paper) | ISBN 9781620318331 (paperback)
Subjects: LCSH: Fourth of July—Juvenile literature. | Fourth of July celebrations—Juvenile literature.
Classification: LCC E286 (ebook) | LCC E286 .A13937 2017 (print) | DDC 394.2634—dc23
LC record available at https://lccn.loc.gov/2017022925

Editors: Jenny Fretland VanVoorst & Jenna Trnka
Book Designer: Leah Sanders
Photo Researcher: Leah Sanders

Photo Credits: busypix/iStock, cover; KidStock/Getty, 1, 11, 23ml; Picture Partners/Alamy, 3; Milleflore Images/Shutterstock, 4; Africa Studio/Shutterstock, 5, 23tr; Ariel Skelley/Getty, 6–7; Gene Bleile/Shutterstock, 8–9, 22tr; Cory A Ulrich/Shutterstock, 10; LauriPatterson/Getty, 12–13; Gino Santa Maria/Shutterstock, 14–15, 22bl; Ryan McVay/Getty, 16, 23br; Naaman Abreu/Shutterstock, 17, 22br, 23bl; Flaffy/Shutterstock, 18–19; kali9/iStock, 20–21, 23tl; Leonard Zhukovsky/Shutterstock, 22tl; pavalena/Shutterstock, 23mr; Creativeye99/iStock, 24.

Printed in the United States of America at Corporate Graphics in North Mankato, Minnesota.

Table of Contents

What Is Independence Day?

It is Independence Day!

It is a U.S. holiday.

4

It is July 4.

We call it the Fourth of July.

What do we celebrate?
Freedom!

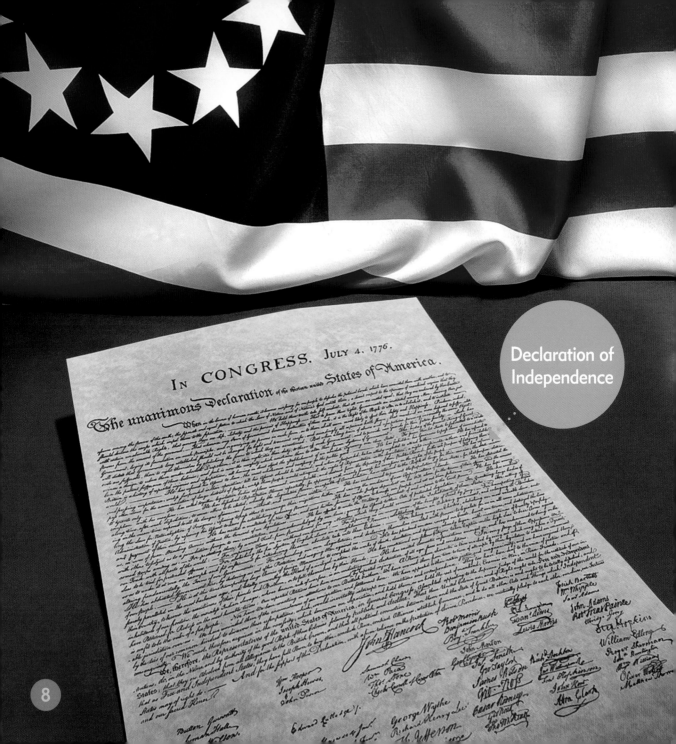

Declaration of
Independence

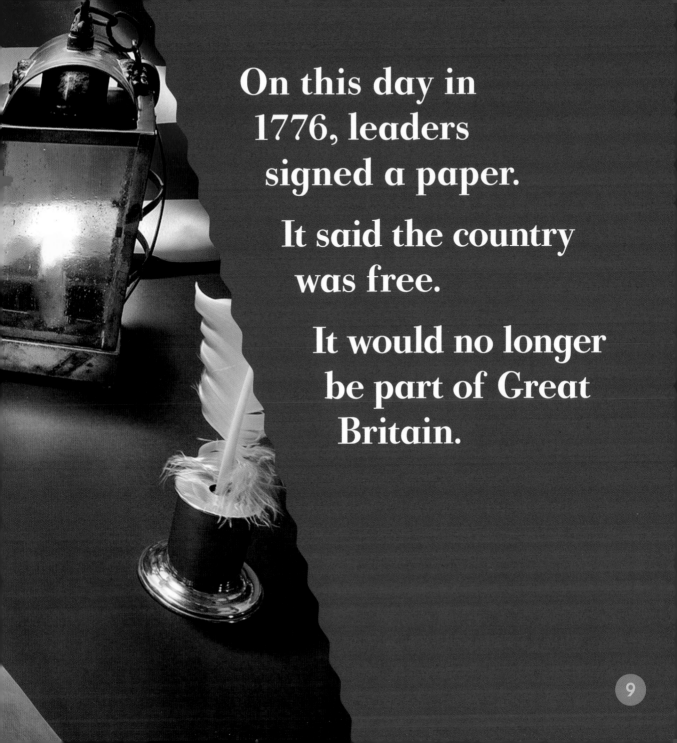

On this day in 1776, leaders signed a paper.

It said the country was free.

It would no longer be part of Great Britain.

How do we celebrate?
We fly the flag.

flag

10

We wear its colors.

What are they?

Red, white, and blue.

We have picnics.

We watch
fireworks.

Pretty!

**Cities hold parades.
Marching bands play.**

Floats drive by.

We make festive snacks.
They are red and blue.
Yum!

Happy Fourth of July!

Symbols of Independence Day

American flag
A symbol of the United States.

fireworks
Loud, explosive devices that burst in the sky and display bright colors.

Declaration of Independence
The document the country's leaders signed to declare independence from Great Britain.

parade
A large public way to celebrate a special event.

Picture Glossary

celebrate
To observe in a special way.

freedom
The state of being independent and not under the power of another.

festive
Relating to a holiday.

Great Britain
A group of nations in Europe that controlled the American colonies in 1776.

floats
Vehicles or trailers decorated for a parade.

marching bands
Bands that march while playing instruments.

Index

To Learn More

Learning more is as easy as 1, 2, 3.

1) Go to www.factsurfer.com

2) Enter "IndependenceDay" into the search box.

3) Click the "Surf" button to see a list of websites.

With factsurfer.com, finding more information is just a click away.

24